Progressive Recorder

Method for Young Beginners

Book 1

By Andrew Scott and Gary Turner
Illustrated by James Stewart

Let's Practice Together

We have recorded all the songs in this book (see the front of this book for more details). When your teacher is not there, instead of practicing by yourself, you can play along with us. Practicing will be more fun and you will learn much quicker.

 ← This icon with a number indicates that a recorded example is available.

Practice the examples on your own, playing slowly at first. Then try playing with a metronome set to a slow tempo, until you can play the example evenly and without stopping. Gradually increase the tempo as you become more confident and then you can try playing along with the recordings. To play along with the recordings your instrument must be in tune.

 Visit our Website
www.learntoplaymusic.com

 Contact us via email
info@learntoplaymusic.com

 Like us on Facebook
www.facebook.com/LearnToPlayMusic

 Follow us on Twitter
twitter.com/LTPMusic

 View our YouTube Channel
www.youtube.com/learntoplaymusiccom

Published by
KOALA MUSIC PUBLICATIONS™

PROGRESSIVE RECORDER METHOD
FOR YOUNG BEGINNERS - BOOK 1
ISBN: 978-0-947183-37-0
Order Code: 18337

Contents

Introduction   **Page 4**
How to Tune Your Recorder   4

Lesson 1   **Page 5**
How to Hold the Recorder   5
How to Make a Sound   6
Tonguing   6
Taking Breaths   6
How to Read Music   7
The Quarter Note   7
The Note B   8
B Happy   **8**
The Four Four Time Signature   8
Four Busy Bees   **9**
The Quarter Note Rest   9
Take a Rest   **9**
Forty-Four Bees   **9**

Lesson 2   **Page 10**
The Note A   10
The A Train   **10**
Repeat Signs   10
B a Friend   **10**
The Half Note   11
Half a Bee   **11**
B Hive Yourself   **11**
Half Time   **11**

Lesson 3   **Page 12**
The Note G   12

G Wiz   **12**
Be a Giraffe   **12**
Three Giraffes   **13**
Sister Giraffe   **13**
The Half Note Rest   13
Toot, Toot   **13**
Merrily   **14**
In the Light of the Moon   **14**

Lesson 4   **Page 15**
The Note C   15
Four Cool Cats   **15**
Easy to C   **15**
Good Evening Friends   **16**
C the Circus   **16**

Lesson 5   **Page 17**
The Note D   17
D - licious   **17**
D - lightful   **17**
Mary Had a Little Lamb   **18**
Go Tell Aunt Nancy   **18**
Aura Lee   **19**
Oats and Beans   **19**
The Common Time Signature   20
Ode to Joy   **20**
Lightly Row   **20**

Lesson 6   **Page 21**
The Three Four Time Signature   21

Opera House Waltz   **21**
Waltz and All   **21**
Austrian Waltz   **22**
Boating Song   **22**

Lesson 7   **Page 23**
Dots   23
Roses from the South   **23**
Girls and Boys Come Out to Play   **24**
Little Bo Peep   **24**

Lesson 8   **Page 25**
The Lead-In   25
The Cuckoo   **25**
Mexican Hat Dance   **26**

Lesson 9   **Page 27**
Staccato   27
Hot Cross Buns   **27**
Toot and Tap   **27**

Lesson 10   **Page 28**
The Whole Note   28
See-Saw Song   **28**
Banks of the Ohio   **29**
When the Saints Go Marchin' In   **30**
Notes and Rest Values   32

Introduction

Progressive Recorder Method for Young Beginners Books 1, 2 & 3 have been designed to introduce the younger student to the basics of recorder playing and reading music. To maximise the student's enjoyment and interest, the Progressive Young Beginner Series incorporates an extensive repertoire of well-known childrens' songs.

All the songs have been carefully graded into an easy-to-follow, lesson-by-lesson format, which assumes no prior knowledge of music or the recorder by the student. Chord symbols for guitar and piano accompaniment are provided for each song.

Book 1 uses very easy arrangements involving five notes with the left hand. It introduces the student to $\frac{4}{4}$ and $\frac{3}{4}$ time, and incorporates quarter, half and whole notes and their equivalent rests. The student is taught how to read music, and introduced to basic terms such as bar lines, repeat signs and lead-in notes. New pieces of information are highlighted by color boxes, and color illustrations are used throughout to stimulate and maintain the student's interest.

How to Tune Your Recorder

To play along with the exercises on the recording, your recorder must be in tune with the recorder on the recording. Tune the B note of your recorder to the first exercise using the following steps. You may need your teacher to help you.

Step 1 Move the mouthpiece of your recorder so that there is a gap of about one quarter of an inch (6mm) between the mouth piece and the body of the recorder. Play the B note on the recording, and then play a B note on your recorder. If the recording sounds the same as your recorder, you are in luck because your recorder is already in tune.

Step 2 If the recording sounds LOWER (or flat) use a twisting action to pull the mouthpiece about one sixteenth of an inch (2mm) **further out**. This will make your recorder sound a bit lower. Check to see if it is now in tune with the recording. If not, try again.

Step 3 If the recording sounds HIGHER (or sharp) use a twisting action to push the mouthpiece about one sixteenth of an inch (2mm) **further in**. This will make your recorder sound a bit higher. Check to see if it is now in tune with the recording. If not try again.
Blowing harder makes a note sound higher, so try to blow each note gently and evenly.

Summary
To make the recorder sound sharper, or higher, make it shorter.
To make the recorder sound flatter, or lower make it longer.

Lesson 1

How to Hold the Recorder

Left Hand

Left Thumb LT

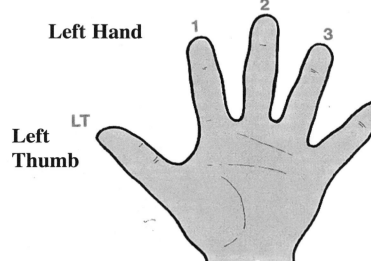

Right Hand

Right Thumb

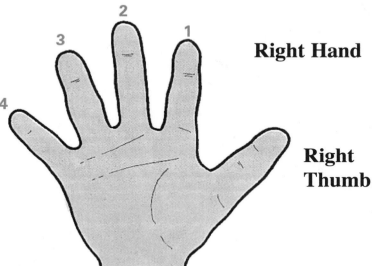

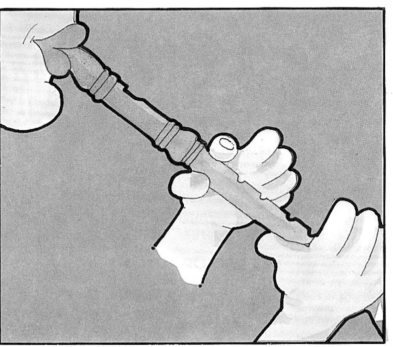

Place the first finger of your left hand on the round hole at the top of the recorder. Look at the picture to make sure you have your finger in the right place.

Place the thumb of your left hand on the hole at the back of the recorder. Let your right hand thumb support the recorder for every note. **You are now fingering the note B**.

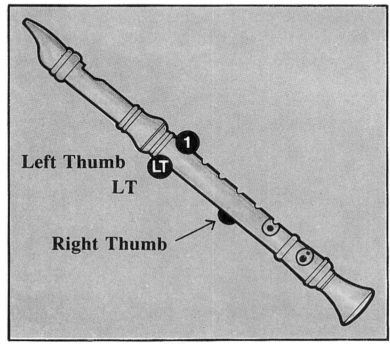

Left Thumb LT

Right Thumb

How to Make a Sound

Holding the note B, blow gently into the mouthpiece. You are now playing a B note. If you blow too hard, the recorder will make a squeaking sound. Try to blow smoothly and steadily so that the note sounds clear.

Tonguing

Without the recorder in your mouth, say the word 'too'. Say it again in a whisper without using your voice. Now with the recorder in your mouth, play some B notes. Say 'too' to start each note. This is called tonguing.

Taking Breaths

When playing songs, you will need to take breaths.

❜ This is a breathmark.

When you see one of these, take a gentle breath through your mouth.
Keep the recorder against your bottom lip.
Do not breathe in through the recorder.

How to Read Music

Music Notes

There are only seven letters used for notes in music. They are:

These notes are known as the **musical alphabet.**

The Staff

These five lines are called the **staff** or **stave**.

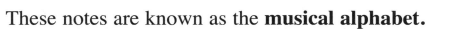

The Quarter Note

This is a musical note called a **quarter note**. Sometimes called a **crotchet**.

The Treble Clef

This symbol is called a **treble clef**. There is a treble clef at the beginning of every line of guitar music.

Music notes are written in the spaces and on the lines of the staff.

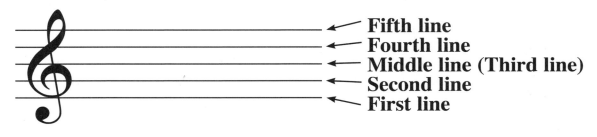

← **Fifth line**
← **Fourth line**
← **Middle line (Third line)**
← **Second line**
← **First line**

The Note B

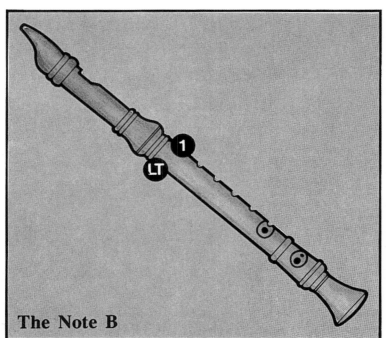

B note

This is a **B** note. The note B is placed on the middle line of the staff.

The Note B

 **1 - B Happy**

On pages 5 and 6 you learnt how to play the B note. In your first song, called **B Happy**, there are eight B notes. Play four B notes, then take a breath (❜) and play four more. **The letters above the staff are chord symbols for piano or guitar players to play along with you**.

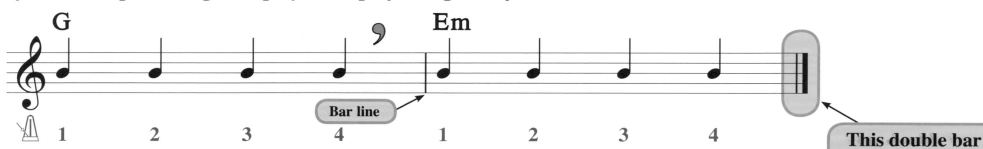

Bar line

1   2   3   4   1   2   3   4

Music is divided into **bars**, or **measures**, by **barlines**. In this song there are two bars of music.

This double bar line tells us that the exercise has finished.

The Four Four Time Signature

These two numbers are called the **time signature**.
They are placed after the treble clef.
The $\frac{4}{4}$ time signature tells you that there are **four** counts in each bar.
There are **four** quarter notes in each bar of four four time.

2 - Four Busy Bees

The song **Four Busy Bees** is in 4/4 time. There are four counts in each bar. Remember to take a breath between each bar. Count each note in your head while you are playing. Remember to blow gently and tongue each note.

The Quarter Note Rest

 This symbol is called a **quarter note rest**. Sometimes called a **crotchet rest**. It means there is **one** count of silence.
Do not play any note. We place **small counting numbers** under rests.

Count: 1

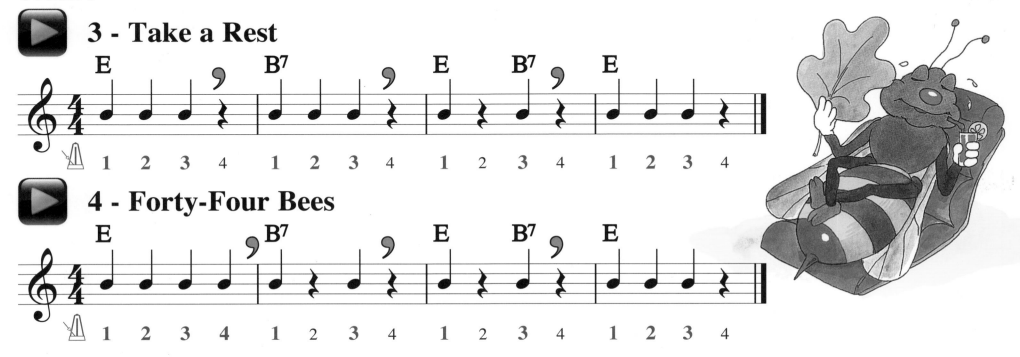

3 - Take a Rest

4 - Forty-Four Bees

Lesson 2

The Note A

The note **A** is placed in the **second** space of the staff.

← Fourth space
← Third space
← Second space
← First space

A note

To play the A note, use the **thumb, first** and **second** fingers of your left hand.

The Note A

5 - The A Train

A   D⁷   A   D⁷   A

1 2 3 4   1 2 3 4   1 2 3 4   1 2 3 4

These two dots are called a **repeat sign**. This means that you play the song again from the start.

6 - B A Friend

Bm   A   Bm   A   Bm

1 2 3 4   1 2 3 4   1 2 3 4   1 2 3 4

The Half Note

This symbol is a **half note**. Sometimes called a **minim**. It lasts for **two** counts. There are only two half notes in one bar of $\frac{4}{4}$ time.

Count: 1   2

Count: 1   2

7 - Half A Bee

This song contains four bars of half notes, using B and A.

G   Am   Bm   Am   G

1   2   3   4   1   2   3   4   1   2   3   4   1   2   3   4

The **big** numbers **1** and **3** tell you to play the note. The **small** numbers 2 and 4 tell you to hold until the next note.

8 - B Hive Yourself

Dmaj⁷ Gmaj⁷ Dmaj⁷ Gmaj⁷ Dmaj⁷ Gmaj⁷ Dmaj⁷ Gmaj⁷

1   2   3   4   1   2   3   4   1   2   3   4   1   2   3   4

9 - Half Time

G   D⁷   G   D⁷   G   D⁷   D⁷   G

1   2   3   4   1   2   3   4   1   2   3   4   1   2   3   4

Squeaks and Squawks

If your recorder makes funny squeaking noises instead of proper notes, here is what you should do:

1. Make sure your fingers cover the holes completely.
2. Blow gently and smoothly.

Lesson 3

The Note G

G note

To play the note **G**, use the **thumb**, **first**, **second** and **third** fingers of your left hand.

The Note G

10 - G Wiz

C   Am   Dm   G⁷

1 2 3 4   1 2 3 4   1 2 3 4   1 2 3 4

11 - B A Giraffe

G   D⁷   G   D⁷   G   D⁷   G

1 2 3 4   1 2 3 4   1 2 3 4   1 2 3 4

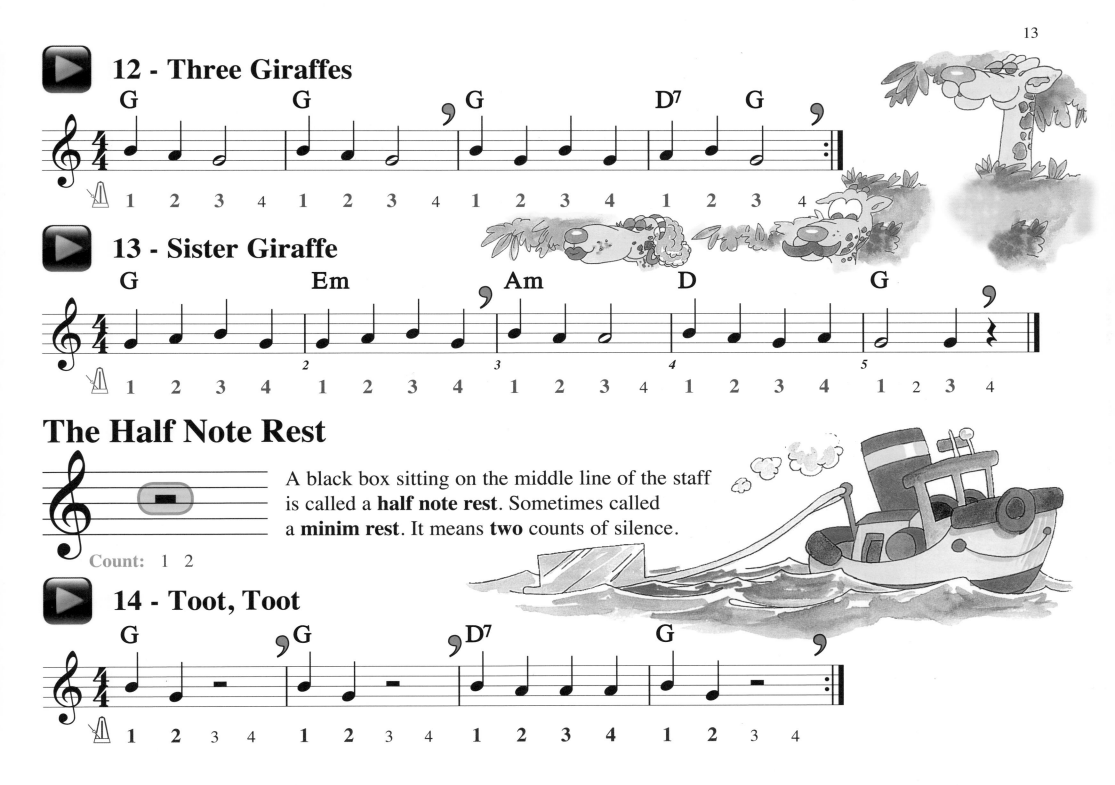

14

15 - Merrily

Traditional

G　　　　　　　　G　　　　　　　D⁷　　　　　　G

Mer - ri - ly　we　roll　a - long,　roll　a - long,　roll　a - long.

G　　　　　　　　G　　　　　　　D⁷　　　　　　G

Mer - ri - ly　we　roll　a - long　o - ver　deep　blue　seas.

16 - In the Light of the Moon

Traditional French

G　　　　　　G　　D⁷　G　　D⁷　　G

1　2　3　4　1　2　3　4　1　2　3　4　1　2　3　4

Lesson 4
The Note C

C note

To play the note **C**, use the **thumb** and **second** finger of your left hand.

The Note C

17 - Four Cool Cats

18 - Easy to C

It's so ea-sy, 1, 2, 3, it's so ea-sy A, B, C,

it's so ea-sy Do, Re, Mi. It's so ea-sy as can be.

The note C usually has the stem going downwards.

The stem for the B note can go up or down.

19 - Good Evening Friends

20 - C the Circus

When the cir - cus comes to town, we all will sing and play. And

when the cir - cus comes to town we will be good all day.

Progressive Recorder
Method for Young Beginners

The Note F#

The Note G

The Note A

The Note D

The Note E

The Note F

Dotted Half Note	Whole Note
𝅗𝅥.	𝅝
𝄼	▬
3	4

ACCIDENTALS

Flat	♭	A flat sign before a note **lowers** the pitch of the note by one **semitone** or one **half step**.
Sharp	♯	A sharp sign before a note **raises** the pitch of the note by one **semitone** or one **half step**.
Natural	♮	A natural sign **cancels** the effect of a sharp or flat for the rest of that bar or until another sharp or flat sign occurs within that bar.

KoalaMusic™

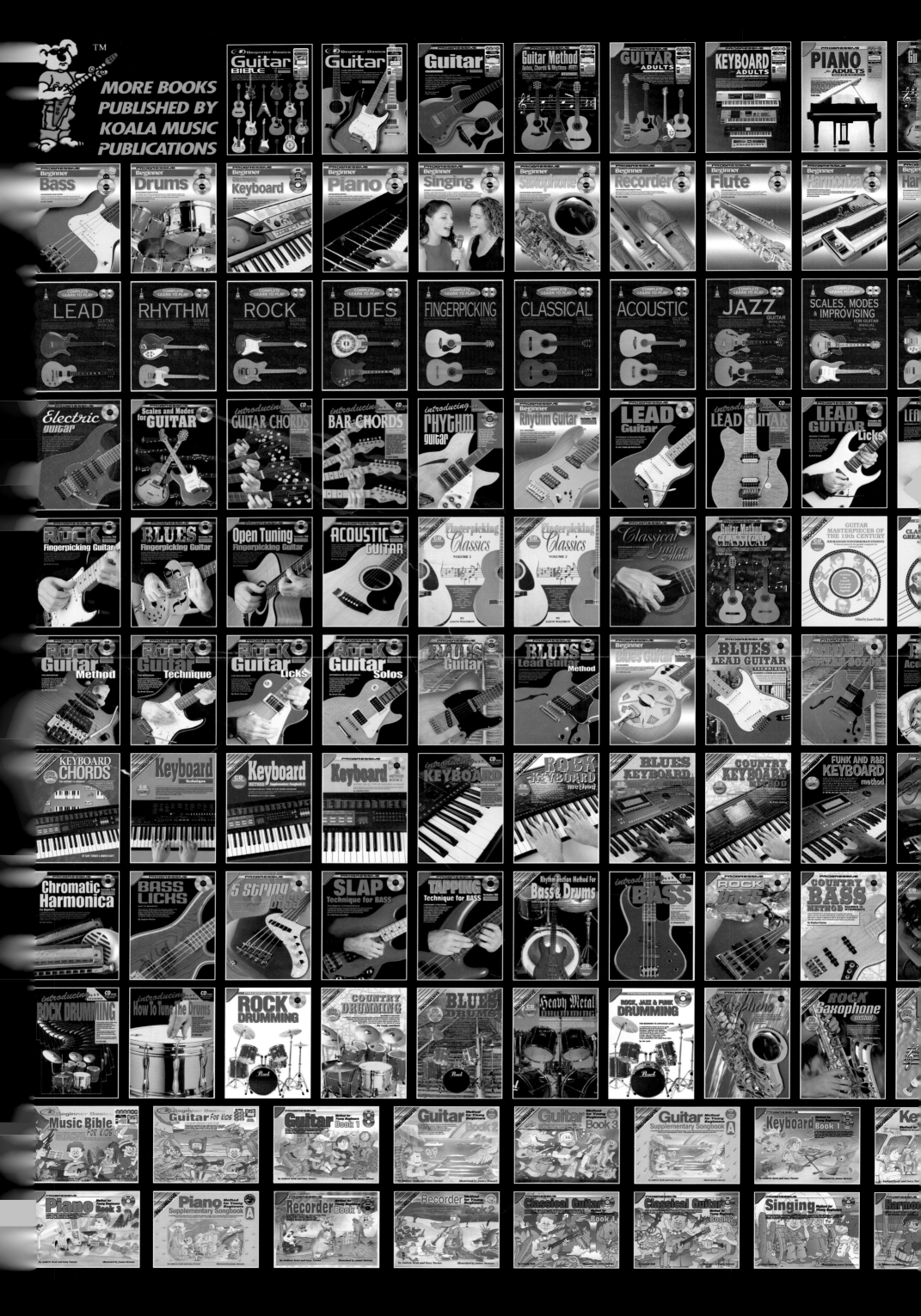

MORE BOOKS
PUBLISHED BY
KOALA MUSIC
PUBLICATIONS

MUSIC ALPHABET

A B C D E F G

The Note C

leger
line

The Note D

The Note E

The Note B

The Note B♭

The Note C

NOTES AND RESTS

Name	Eighth Notes	Quarter Note	Dotted Quarter Note	Half Note
Note	♪	♩	♩.	♪
Rest	𝄾	𝄽	𝄽.	▬
Number of Counts	+	1	1 +	2

TIME SIGNATURES

4/4 Four counts in each bar.

3/4 Three counts in each bar.

Lesson 5

The Note D

D note

To play the note **D**, use the **second** finger of your left hand only. Your right hand thumb helps to support the recorder.

The Note D

21 - D - licious

22 - D - lightful

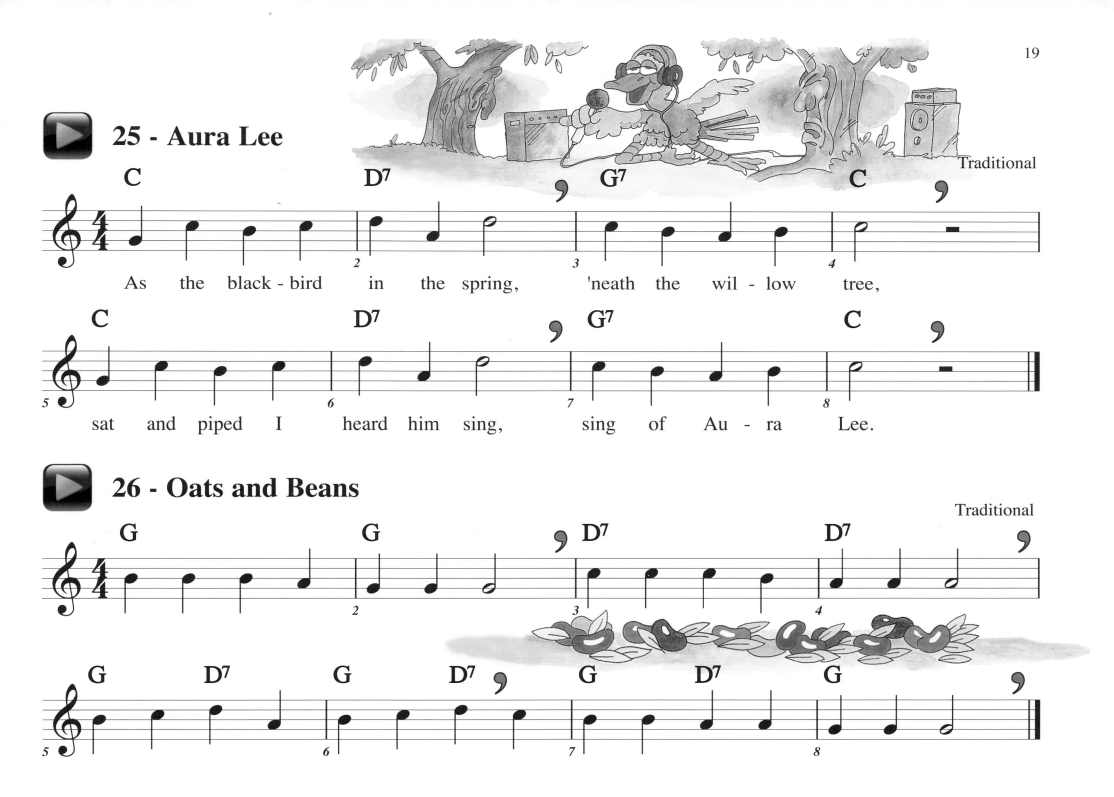

25 - Aura Lee

Traditional

As the black-bird in the spring, 'neath the wil-low tree,

sat and piped I heard him sing, sing of Au-ra Lee.

26 - Oats and Beans

Traditional

The Common Time Signature

C This symbol is called **common time**.
It means exactly the same as $\frac{4}{4}$.

27 - Ode to Joy

Ludwig van Beethoven

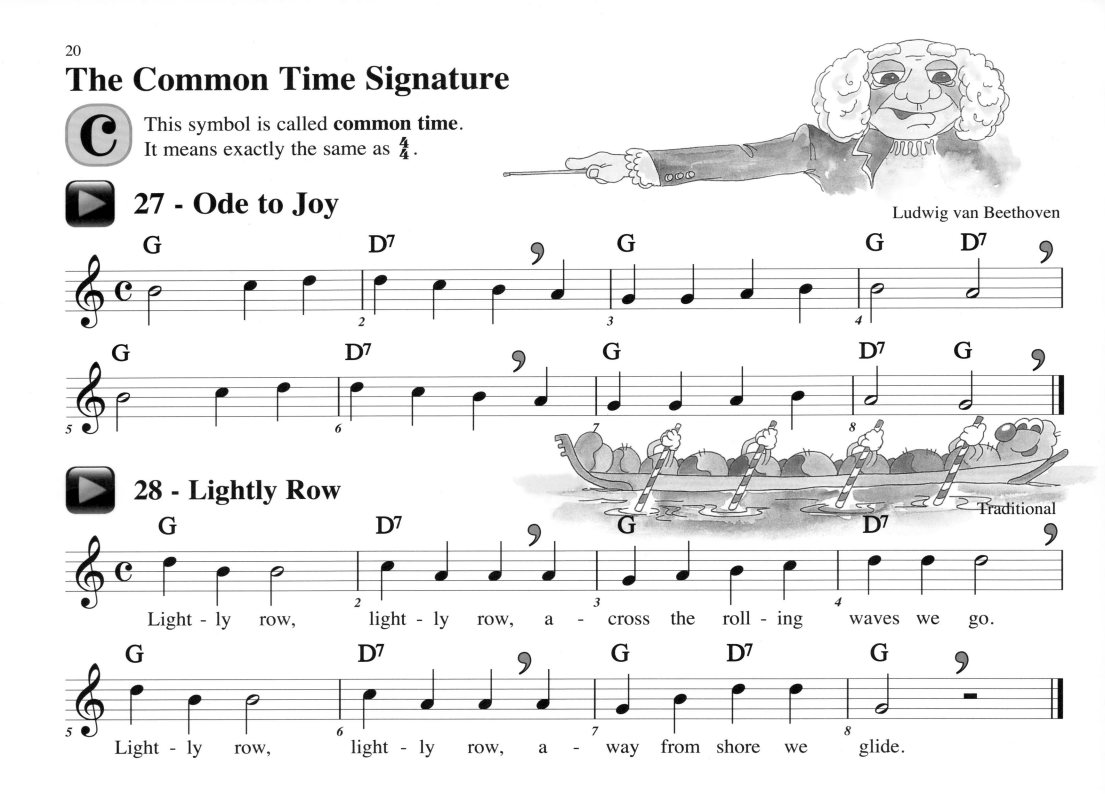

28 - Lightly Row

Traditional

Light - ly row, light - ly row, a - cross the roll - ing waves we go.

Light - ly row, light - ly row, a - way from shore we glide.

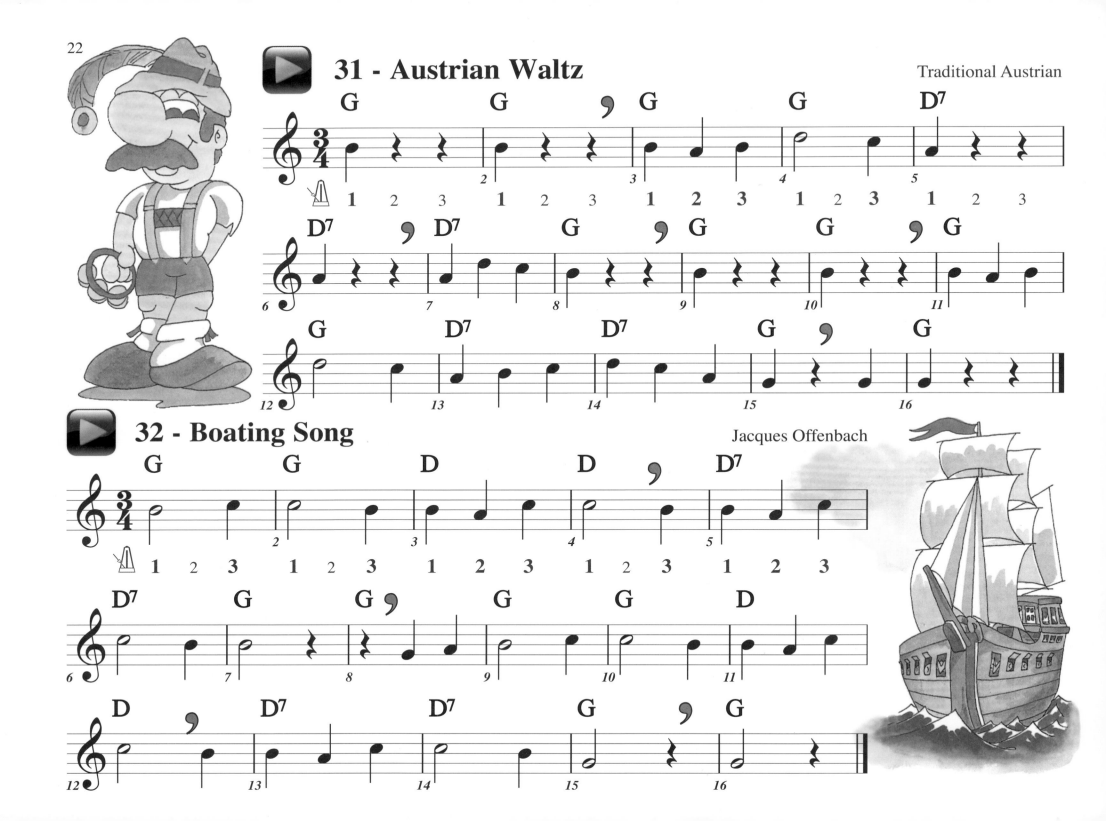

Lesson 7

Dots

A **dot** placed after a half note means that you hold the note for **three** counts. One dotted half note makes one bar of music in **¾** time. This note is called a **dotted half note** or **dotted minim**.

Count: **1** 2 3

The Dotted Half Note

Count: **1** 2 3

33 - Roses from the South

Johann Strauss

On the recording there are **three** drumbeats to introduce this song.

34 - Girls and Boys Come Out to Play
Traditional

Girls and boys come out to play, the
moon is shin ___ ing bright as day.

35 - Little Bo Peep
Traditional

Lit - tle Bo Peep has lost her sheep and does - n't know
where ___ to find them. Leave them a - lone, and they will come
home, bring - ing their tails ___ be - hind them.

Lesson 8

The Lead-in (or Pick-up)

Sometimes a song does not begin on the first beat of a bar. Any notes which come before the first full bar are called **lead-in notes** **(or pick-up notes)**. When we use lead-in notes, the last bar is also incomplete. The notes in the lead-in and the notes in the last bar add up to one full bar.

36 - The Cuckoo

On the recording there are **five** drumbeats to introduce this song.

37 - Mexican Hat Dance

On the recording there are
five drumbeats to introduce this song.

Traditional Mexican

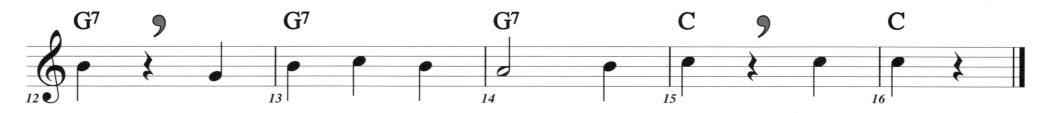

Lesson 9

Staccato

A **dot** placed below or above a note tells you to play the note **staccato**. Staccato means to play the note **short and separate** from other notes. To play a note short, make a '**t**' sound with your tongue instead of the 'too' sound.

38 - Hot Cross Buns

Traditional

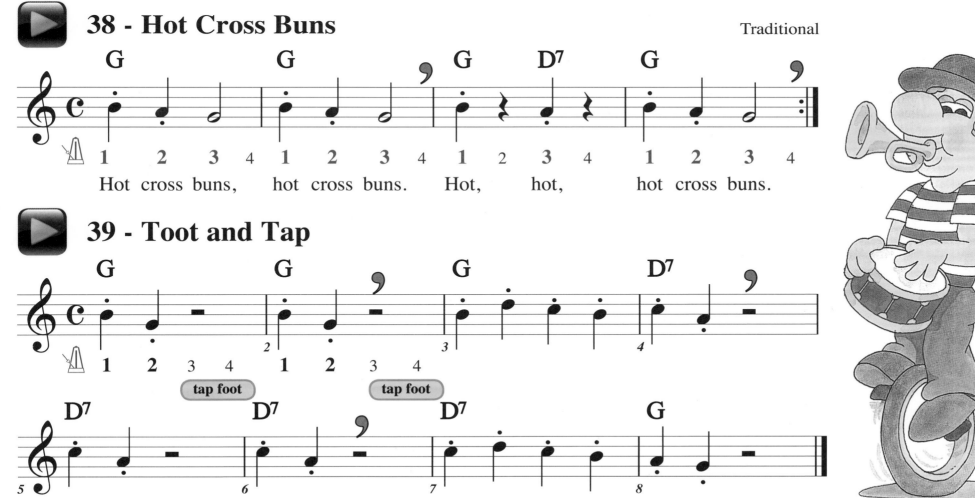

Hot cross buns,   hot cross buns.   Hot,   hot,   hot cross buns.

39 - Toot and Tap

tap foot   tap foot

Lesson 10

The Whole Note

Count: **1** 2 3 4

This is a **whole** note. Sometimes called a **semibreve**. It lasts for **four** counts.

Count: 1   2   3   4

 40 - See - Saw Song

41 - Banks of the Ohio

On the recording there are **five** drumbeats to introduce this song.

Traditional

42 - When the Saints Go Marchin' In

On the recording there are **five** drumbeats to introduce this song.

Traditional

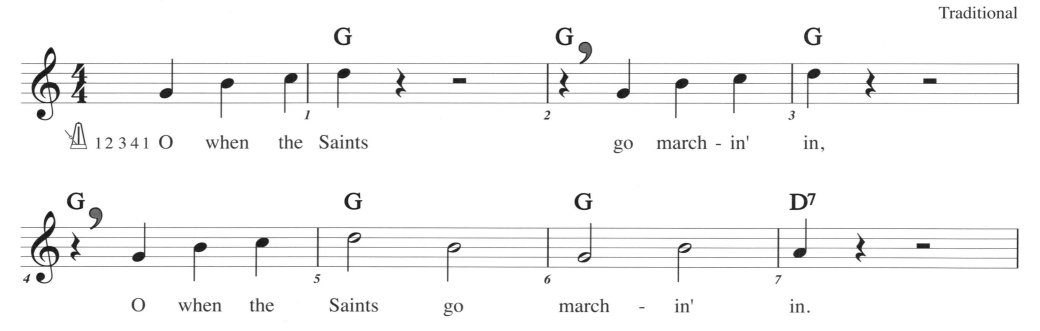

1 2 3 4 1 O when the Saints go march-in' in,

O when the Saints go march - in' in.

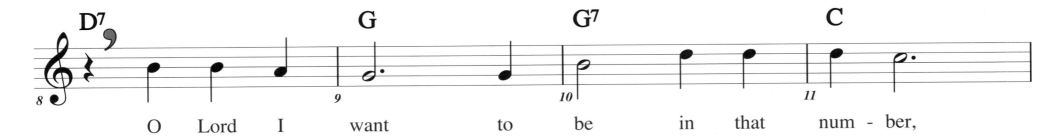

O Lord I want to be in that num - ber,

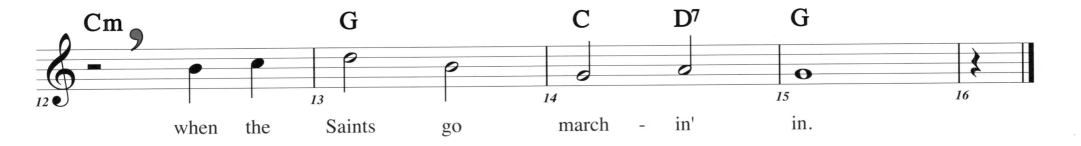

when the Saints go march - in' in.

Note and Rest Values

Name	Quarter Note	Half Note	Dotted Half Note	Whole Note
Note	♩	♩	♩.	𝅝
Rest	𝄽	▬	▬ 𝄽	▬
Number of Counts	1	2	3	4

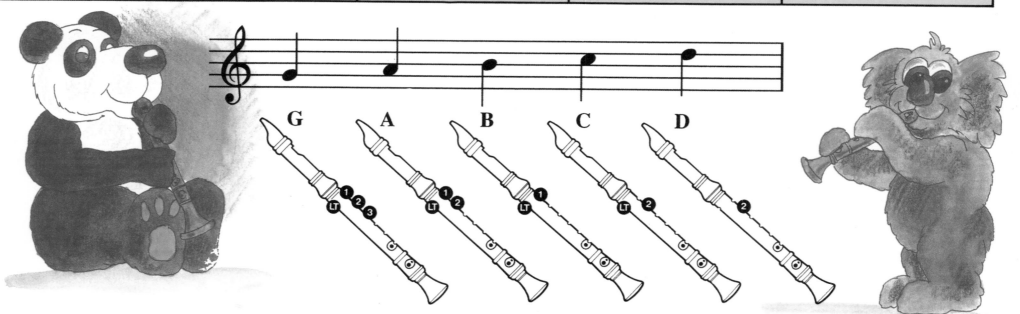

Congratulations on completing book 1. Now proceed to book 2.